A LIFE
Exalted

June Kimmel

Greenville, South Carolina

Front and Back Cover Photo Credits: Brand X Pictures

The fact that materials produced by other publishers may be referred to in this volume does not constitute an endorsement of the content or theological position of materials produced by such publishers.

All Scripture is quoted from the Authorized King James Version.

A Life Exalted
June Kimmel

Design by Rita Golden
Composition by Kelley Moore

© 2007 by BJU Press
Greenville, South Carolina 29614

Printed in the United States of America
All rights reserved

ISBN 978-1-59166-730-8

15   14   13   12   11   10   9   8   7   6   5   4   3   2   1

With love to Mom and Dad

Audrey Balcom Towne
and
Clifford E. Balcom
(1925–80)

Who introduced me to the Savior
and to the joy of
sharing Him with others

TABLE OF CONTENTS

A LIFE SURRENDERED,
A LIFE EXALTED

Lesson 1
A LIFE SURRENDERED: A REVIEW

Philippians 2:5–8

Let this mind be in you, which was also in Christ
Jesus: who, being in the form of God, thought it not
robbery to be equal with God: but made himself of no
reputation, and took upon him the form of a servant,
and was made in the likeness of men: and being found
in fashion as a man, he humbled himself, and became
obedient unto death, even the death of the cross.

A Life Surrendered looked at Philippians 2:5–8 in depth. *A Life Exalted* will continue the study of what Jesus' surrender means to each of us. We will go beyond His submission to see how God the Father exalted Jesus because of His life and sacrifice for us. This brief review is a reminder of how the Lord Jesus clearly depicted a surrendered life.

Who Being God

Time in the Word: Read John 1:1–5; 17:5, 24.

The Lord Jesus is God—a truth upon which all we believe rests. He didn't begin His existence as a baby in Bethlehem's stable. Jesus for eternity past was in heaven as our eternal God, Creator, and promised Redeemer. He knows a perfect relationship of unity and love with

God the Father and God the Holy Spirit. He willingly surrendered to redemption's plan by leaving behind the glories of heaven, coming to this earth as man, and becoming our Savior.

1. Summarize what you learned about Jesus from these verses.

Passage	Who Jesus Is
John 1:1	
John 1:3	
John 17:5	
John 17:24	

Let This Mind Be in You

2. Is He worthy of your surrender?_____

What areas do you still find difficult to surrender to Him?_____

_____

_____

_____

_____

Made in the Likeness of Man

When Jesus came to this earth, He not only took on the form of man but He also became man yet remained God. Only the Son of God could bridge the gap that sin had made between man and God. He surrendered to the process of birth and the stages of growth. He surrendered to a life of simplicity in order for Him to be our sympathetic and compassionate High Priest, Who is touched with the pain and struggles of our infirmities.

Read Luke 2:40, 52 to answer the following questions to be reminded of what Jesus experienced as a man.

3. How do these verses describe Jesus' growth as a boy?

Verse 40

a. _____

_____

b. _____

_____

c. _____

_____

Verse 52

a. _____

_____

b. _____

_____

c. _____

_____

4. What human characteristics do theses verses say Jesus had?

Matthew 25:35_____

_____

Matthew 26:12_____

_____

Matthew 26:38_____

_____

Mark 4:38_____

_____

5. Does He truly understand your struggles and pain? How should
this encourage you?

_____

_____

_____

_____

Made Himself of No Reputation

Jesus lived a life of humility. Being reared in the home of a carpenter,
He learned the skills of the trade while He worked by Joseph's side.
He probably labored there for eighteen years—each day prepared
Him for the demanding years of ministry that would follow.

Jesus ministered with humility. He had not come to overthrow
the Roman government and establish an earthly kingdom. Nor was
He part of the religious governing bodies. The Lord Jesus ministered
to those around Him in a quiet, unassuming way, dealing with individuals even when He was surrounded by masses.

6. Match the examples of the humility Jesus showed in His earthly
ministry with the correct reference.

_____ Matthew 9:10–13   A. Obedient to the Father's will

_____ Matthew 13:55   B. Met people where they were
                                 in order to minister to them

_____ Luke 22:27   C. Known as a carpenter's son

_____ John 5:30   D. Came to serve

_____ I Corinthians 8:9   E. Became poor that we might
                                 be rich

7. Are you concerned about recognition for your service?_____

8. What do you gladly do for the Lord that others may not be aware of?_____

_____

Took upon Him the Form of a Servant

Read John 13:2–14, focusing on how Jesus approached His ministry with the heart of a servant. Often His disciples would vie for recognition and status, but Jesus continually brought them back to the reality of effective ministry found in serving each other. Jesus gave the ultimate example of servant-leadership when He ate the Passover meal with the disciples. He set for His disciples and for each of us a picture of true ministry—lovingly caring for the needs of others.

9. How did Jesus show His servant's heart to His disciples?_____

_____

_____

10. How do you display the heart of a servant to those around you?

_____

_____

_____

Obedient unto Death

Throughout His ministry, Jesus often sought times of solitude to rest and pray. This time alone with His heavenly Father gave Him the strength for the challenges He faced. Knowing His time of death was fast approaching, Jesus went to the Garden of Gethsemane to spend time in prayer to prepare His heart for what lay ahead. It was in the quietness of this garden that His intense struggle took place. Satan made one last all-out effort to alter redemption's plan. In spite of the agonizing temptations He faced, Jesus proclaimed with confidence, "Not my will, but thine be done." With these words, He declared His full surrender to the will of God the Father.

11. Read Matthew 26:36–46 and list the phrases from Jesus' prayer that indicate His surrender to the Father's will for Him to die on the cross._____

_____

_____

12. What has God asked you to do that, in spite of your fears, you obeyed and did?_____

_____

_____

_____

Let This Mind Be in You

We are ready to begin our study of *A Life Exalted*. We will look at the death, burial, and resurrection of the Lord Jesus and how He exemplified a surrendered life. He gave to us a pattern to follow and a path to walk. The final lessons will show us how God the Father exalted Him and how He asks each of us to do the same. May the Lord challenge your heart to be completely surrendered to Him. May this study lead you to live a life totally surrendered to Him—a life committed to exalting your Lord and Savior.

Time for Prayer: Spend some time in prayer asking the Lord to show you the areas of your life that He would have you surrender to Him.

Time to Memorize: Review Philippians 2:5–8 and then begin to memorize Philippians 2:9–11.

OBEDIENT UNTO DEATH

Lesson 2
THE SURRENDER
TO BETRAYAL

Philippians 2:8
And being found in fashion as a man, he humbled himself,
and became obedient unto death, even the death of the cross.

In the Garden of Gethsemane Jesus had been in prayer for several agonizing hours. He knew what lay ahead. He knew that your salvation and mine depended on Him fulfilling the designed plan of redemption. After Jesus fully surrendered to the will of God the Father, He went to the disciples one last time and found them sleeping again. He told them this time to arise. He knew His betrayer was almost there. Jesus, no doubt, could have seen Judas and the band coming toward Him. Between the light of the full Passover moon and of the blazing torches, the group could not have made its approach unseen this dark night. I wonder how long Jesus sat and watched this diverse band of possibly six hundred Roman soldiers and Jewish temple police. He knew their mission and He knew their leader.

Surrender to the Betrayal of a Friend

Time in the Word: Read Matthew 26:42–56.

After reading Matthew 26:42–56, answer the following questions about Jesus' betrayal.

1. What arrangements had Judas made to identify Who Jesus was (verse 48)?_____

_____

_____

2. What title did Judas call Jesus (verse 49)?_____

_____

3. What did Jesus call Judas in return (verse 50)?_____

_____

4. With the knowledge Jesus had of Judas's intent, why is it so amazing that Jesus referred to Judas with this term?_____

_____

_____

5. How does this encounter with Judas fulfill these Old Testament verses?

   Psalm 41:9_____

   _____

   Psalm 55:12–13_____

   _____

Surrender to Arrest

John records in John 18:4–6 that Jesus asked the soldiers whom they were seeking. Their reply was "Jesus of Nazareth." Jesus acknowledged, "I am He." As He said these words, all that heard Him "fell to the ground" (verse 6). These words were familiar to Jewish ears. Many times throughout the history of the Hebrew people, God had referred to Himself as "I AM." This name "demonstrates His identity with Yahweh in the Old Testament, who was first revealed to Moses as 'I am that I am'" in Exodus 3:14.[1] "I AM," revealed the all-encompassing sufficiency of God. All the needs we face are met in "I AM." Seven times in the book of John Jesus refers to Himself as "I AM" and through this term reveals Himself to us.

6. Read the following passages and match them to the correct "I AM."

_____ John 6:35	A. I am the Light of the World
_____ John 8:12	B. I am the Good Shepherd
_____ John 10:9	C. I am the Vine
_____ John 10:11	D. I am the Bread of Life
_____ John 11:25	E. I am the Resurrection and the Life
_____ John 14:6	F. I am the Door
_____ John 15:5	G. I am the Way, the Truth, and the Life

Touched by the Master's Hand

Read Matthew 26:51–56 and Luke 22:50–51. Even in the midst of this horrific arrest, Jesus never lost sight of the individuals around Him. When Peter impulsively drew his sword and cut off the ear of one of the high priest's servants, Jesus rebuked Peter for his rash behavior and reminded him that with just a word He could call legions of heavenly hosts to rescue Him. To have altered the events of the night would have left the prophecies of previous centuries unfilled. What was happening was all part of God's perfect plan.

Although the other gospels record this incident, only Luke, the physician, tells about Jesus healing the man's ear (Luke 22:38). Think for a minute about this servant, Malchus, whose ear was restored. Do you think he left the garden with the same opinion of Jesus that he had entered with? Do you think he went ahead and aided in Jesus' arrest, trial, and death? I realize the Scripture is silent on this, but I wonder if Jesus could have healed this man's ear and he not believe? Which of us is the same after being truly touched by the Master's hand?

Consider the lives of some Bible characters who were touched by the Lord Jesus. Some of them were touched literally by His loving hands. Others were transformed by His power or through one of the apostles touching their lives.

7. Note the condition of these individuals before and after they were touched by the Master's hand.

Passage	Person(s)	Condition Before	Condition After
Matthew 9:27–31	Two Men		
Mark 10:13–16		Eager to learn and follow	
Luke 7:11–15			
Luke 8:26–35			
Acts 9:1–16			
Acts 9:32–35			

Let This Mind Be in You

As you read the verses in John about the names of "I AM," did you consider how the Lord Jesus revealed Himself through these names?

8. What needs does He promise to meet in your life because of Who He is? Read the verses again and apply His Names to your own life.

Jesus said, "I AM. . . ."	My Need
John 6:35 The Bread of Life	
John 8:12 The Light of the World	
John 10:9 The Door	
John 10:11 The Good Shepherd	
John 11:25 The Resurrection and the Life	
John 14:6 The Way, the Truth, and the Life	
John 15:5 The Vine	

∾ **Time to Memorize: Continue to review Philippians 2:5–8 and memorize verses 9–11.**

∾ **Time for Prayer: Praise God for the work He's done in your life through His saving touch. Ask Him to show you your needs that He desires to meet through the power of His name.**

From My Heart to Yours

When I think back to many women I've known throughout the years, several come immediately to my mind that could relate with Malchus. Some of their lives had been devastated from their earliest memories. Abuse, neglect, abandonment were the norm for them. Yet, when they came to know Jesus as their Savior, they were changed. There were struggles from the scars that sin had left on their lives, but by the grace of God they were new creatures in Christ

Jesus. Old things were passed away and all things were become new. God's mercy and grace is beyond my comprehension. How He proves His miraculous love over and over in each of our lives!

Jesus knew that this betrayal and arrest were necessary steps to Calvary. He knew to fulfill the prophesies of old He must willingly surrender to every aspect of this night. He must follow God's perfect plan of redemption. But even in the vastness of this atonement, He never lost sight of the individual. He died for the whole world. He died for you.

Lesson 3
THE SURRENDER
TO A TRIAL

Philippians 2:8

**And being found in fashion as a man, he humbled himself,
and became obedient unto death, even the death of the cross.**

*W*hen the band of men left the Garden of Gethsemane with the Lord Jesus, they began a night of illegal events that broke countless Roman and Jewish laws. The time of day, the order of the proceedings, and the witnesses violated the current laws, but Jesus never demanded different treatment. He went through that night as Isaiah had predicted—"He is brought as a lamb to the slaughter, and as a sheep before her shearers is dumb, so he openeth not his mouth" (Isaiah 53:7).

Surrender to the Unlawful Acts

∾ **Time in the Word: Read Matthew 26:57–68.**

When the false witnesses hurled their words against Jesus, He kept silent. He did not defend Himself or plead for acquittal. He gave His life; no one would take it from Him. He willingly, defenselessly laid it down. Jesus "maintained the dignified calm, the loving forbearance that had always characterized Him."[1] "His silence was more crushing than a spate of words."[2]

Jesus did answer His accusers other times during this long night when His deity or His doctrines were being questioned. He responded in a manner consistent with Who He was—God in the flesh, Redeemer and King.

Read the following passages and note who was questioning Jesus, their question(s), and Jesus' response.

1. Matthew 26:62–63a

   Accuser_____

   _____

   Question(s) asked_____

   _____

   Jesus' response_____

   _____

2. Matthew 26:63b–64

   Accuser_____

   _____

   Question(s) asked_____

   _____

   Jesus' response_____

   _____

3. Mark 15:2

   Accuser_____

   _____

   Question(s) asked_____

   _____

Jesus' response_____

_____

4. Mark 15:3–5

   Accuser_____

   _____

   Questions(s) asked_____

   _____

   Jesus' response_____

   _____

5. Luke 23:8–9

   Accuser_____

   _____

   Questions(s) asked_____

   _____

   Jesus' response_____

   _____

6. John 18:20–23

   Accuser_____

   _____

   Questions(s) asked_____

   _____

   Jesus' response_____

   _____

7. John 19:10

Accuser_____

_____

Question(s) asked_____

_____

_____

Jesus' response_____

_____

Let This Mind Be in You

In the United States it is difficult to comprehend that countless people around the world live in fear of losing their lives because they are Christians. Our lives are inconvenienced at times because we are saved, but we don't suffer persecution. Someone has noted that many people talk about being willing to die for Christ, but few are willing to live boldly for Him. As Jesus was obedient unto death, you and I need to be obedient not only unto death but unto life as well. He may not ask us to die for Him, but He does ask us to live for Him.

Look at some familiar, but challenging, passages on living for the Lord and see what a surrendered life should be.

Read Romans 12:1–2.

8. How are you to present your body to the Lord?_____

_____

_____

9. How is this different from what is presented in the Old Testament?

_____

_____

10. What will a life lived this way prove?_____

_____

_____

_____

_____

11. What are some practical ways that you can demonstrate this in your daily life?_____

_____

_____

_____

_____

Read I Corinthians 10:31.

12. What areas of your life does this verse address?_____

_____

_____

13. With what attitude are you to do these activities?_____

_____

_____

14. Do you consistently accomplish this in your walk with the Lord? Explain._____

_____

15. What changes do you need to make in your attitudes and/or activities?_____

_____

_____

_____

Read II Corinthians 5:17–21.

16. How should your life be different as a child of God?_____

_____

_____

17. Who are you now to represent?_____

_____

18. Are you doing this by the way you live your life? Explain._____

_____

_____

_____

Read Philippians 1:21.

19. What should be your approach to life?_____

_____

_____

20. What should be your attitude toward death?_____

_____

_____

∼ **Time for Prayer: Spend time with God surrendering your life totally to His will for you. Give Him every aspect of your life. Ask Him to use you as a living sacrifice in loving service to Him.**

∼ **Time to Memorize: Continue to memorize Philippians 2:5–11.**

From My Heart to Yours

We were seated around a large table in a restaurant not far from our church. The missions conference speaker was our guest. My daughter joined our meal already in progress. When we introduced her to the speaker, he asked her a series of questions that very quickly revealed his desire to understand her walk with the Lord and what direction the Lord might be calling her. When asked what she wanted to do after completing high school, she replied with the uncertainty of many teenagers that she didn't know but was praying for God's direction. He realized her openness to follow the Lord's will yet sensed her indecision. Without hesitation, he reached into his pocket for a blank 3 × 5 card and a pen. He held the pen and card over his head and gave us all an illustration to remember. Our lives, he said, are like that blank card. We need to give that card and pen to God for Him to "write" for us the plan He desires us to follow. Nothing prewritten—predetermined—is acceptable. We each must be ready for whatever the Lord asks of us. God's will is personal and complete. Only He can determine what is best for us. But for God's will to be accomplished, we must surrender our lives to Him. We must be willing to be obedient unto life.

Are you totally surrendered to Him? Are you living for Him a life that is clearly surrendered to Him? Or are you holding back in some area? What should you surrender to Him today?

The secret of offering your body to God as a living sacrifice is the transformation of your mind through surrendering your heart totally to Him.

Be obedient unto . . . life.

> Not my will but Thine, Lord;
> Lead me to Calvary.
> Make my life a living sacrifice,
> Crucified for Thee.
>
> —Ron Hamilton[3]

EVEN THE DEATH OF THE CROSS

Lesson 4
THE PROPHECY OF THE CROSS, PART 1

Philippians 2:8
**And being found in fashion as a man, he humbled himself,
and became obedient unto death, even the death of the cross.**

*W*ords seem so insufficient to express the death of the Lord on the cross. This monumental event is beyond my comprehension. Nothing in our world can compare with what took place on that old, rugged cross. Yet, to consider the surrendered life of the Lord Jesus, we must take a close look at the cross to grasp what was accomplished there for us. His arrest and trial clearly portrayed His submission to redemption's plan, but His obedience led Him to a very specific death—death on a Roman cross.

The Prophecy of the Cross

From the very first chapters of Genesis, God began to prepare the world for the Savior that man's sin required. Jesus' death was clearly depicted and prophesied many times throughout the pages of Old Testament history. Through many of the religious observances God was illustrating for His people what would be required to satisfy the debt of sin. Several Old Testament accounts give us a prophetic glimpse of what Jesus accomplished on the cross.

After Adam and Eve sinned in the Garden of Eden, God pronounced the curse of sin that would accompany mankind throughout the ages. Then He cast them from the beautiful garden that He had created for them. Before they left, He replaced the fig leaves that had inadequately covered their nakedness.

1. According to Genesis 3:21, what did God use to make the new covering for Adam and Eve?_____

   _____

2. What would this provision have required of the animal?_____

   _____

   _____

Although the account in Genesis 3 is not detailed as to what God did to provide these coverings for Adam and Eve, God Himself established a precedent. A lamb was slain to provide satisfactory coverings.

In Genesis 4:1–5, we learn of Adam and Eve's sons. When it came time for these adult sons to offer a sacrifice to the Lord, they chose different offerings.

3. Read the verses carefully to compare the brothers' choices.

	Cain	Abel
Genesis 4:1–4 Offerings brought		
Genesis 4:4–5 God's response to offerings		

4. According to Hebrews 9:22 and 11:4, why did God respond as He did to Cain's offering?_____

_____

_____

To Abel's offering?_____

_____

_____

In both of these early accounts, God required a blood sacrifice. The blood that was shed was obtained from an innocent lamb. God was teaching that an offering such as Cain's would not satisfy His demands for the payment of sin; "sin deserved death and could be covered only by the death of a guiltless sacrifice."[1] Cain's beautiful "fruit of the ground" (Genesis 4:3) could not provide the necessary criteria. Cain brought the fruits of his good works, not the requirement acceptable to God.

Another Old Testament account that clearly foreshadows Christ's work on the cross is found in Genesis 22, where we read the account of Abraham's faith being tested when God told him to sacrifice his son Isaac. I marvel at the obedience of Abraham and Isaac. Abraham's heart must have ached as he gathered the necessary things for sacrifice and made that long journey. He perhaps had followed these same paths on previous trips of worship, but this time, with his long-awaited heir as the appointed sacrifice, each step must have pierced his heart. He was confident God would provide, but what must he do before God's provision would be seen.

∾ Time in the Word: Read Genesis 22:1–14.

After carefully reading the account, fill in the blanks to complete the summary of this important event in the life of this father and son.

5. God provided a _____ for Isaac that day and spared the young man's life. The incident gives us an illustration of great significance. _____ had been the one sentenced to die on that _____, but God

sent a _____ lamb. This ram was caught in the _____ by his _____ so that no blemish would mar its body. An innocent _____ gave his life so that _____ life could be spared. That's what Jesus did for us. He, the spotless Lamb of God, willingly took our place on the _____ for all mankind to be spared.

God's payment for sin required the shedding of blood, but no lamb could satisfy the debt of the sin of all mankind. The lamb simply pictured what only Jesus could do. Only the shed blood of the holy, sinless Son of God could pay that overwhelming debt. This practice of offering animal sacrifices would continue throughout Old Testament worship, but when Jesus died on that Roman cross, the debt of sin was satisfied forever.

Let This Mind Be in You

Are you trying to come to God like Cain did—on your own terms instead of His? Answer the following questions to see.

6. Do you willingly obey God's Word?_____

7. Are you easily convicted of sin in your life and have no rest until you confess it to your heavenly Father?_____

8. Do you excuse your sin or ignore it?_____

9. Do you become defensive when you hear preaching about sin that you know is in your life?_____

Are you as willing as Abraham was to give to God whatever He asks? Answer the following questions to see.

10. Do you struggle to have family members involved in ministries that take them away from you?_____

11. Are you willing to be separated from those you love to do the work God has called you to?_____

12. Are you willing to serve God only as long as you can stay within your comfort zone?_____

๛ Time for Prayer: Spend some time in prayer searching your heart. Ask God to show you the areas you want to control and not surrender to Him.

๛ Time to Memorize: Continue to memorize Philippians 2:5–11.

From My Heart to Yours

I've hosted many a Bible study over a cup of tea at my dining room table. Some of the women were eager to learn from God's Word— eagerly feasting on the truths we deliberated over. Others met there with me searching for the answers to their horrible struggle with sins, past and present. Still others would come longing desperately to find anything to even slightly condone the choices they wanted to make.

One young woman who sat at my well-worn table was full of life and energy. She radiated a determination to succeed. She seemed to truly desire to know the truths of God's Word, but mixed with that desire was years of church dogma and rituals. As we studied how the Old Testament points us to the cross, she seemed to be understanding and accepting the truths that God's Word revealed. The day we came to the Ten Commandments, I was hopeful that she would see her inability to reach God's standard of perfection. But to my amazement her response revealed something I hadn't anticipated.

As we went through Moses' famous list of Ten Commandments, she without hesitation disregarded one of them. The rest she said she willingly and actively strove to obey, but this particular one—she couldn't see God being serious about her following it. I was amazed. No amount of explanation on my part would change her mind. She was comfortable working on the other nine to gain God's favor. She saw no need for salvation by faith through grace. Surely nine out of ten would be good enough.

How many of us do the very same thing? We may not approach our disobedience as boldly as my friend did that day, but we still choose what we want to obey from God's Word and set the rest aside.

We may be quick to see the sins of those around us, yet we remain blind to our own lack of surrendered obedience.

How about you? What areas of your life are you holding back from God? Are you willing to obey Him totally? Willing to give up whatever He might ask of you? Willing to apply the truths of His Word to your daily walk?

Ask God right now to show you what He wants you to do to walk in complete obedience to His will. Ask Him to show you the areas of your life that you still want to do your way instead of His.

Lesson 5
THE PROPHECY OF THE CROSS, PART 2

Philippians 2:8
**And being found in fashion as a man, he humbled himself,
and became obedient unto death, even the death of the cross.**

The sacrificial practices of the Old Testament helped the Jewish people to look ahead to the coming of the Lord Jesus and what He would accomplish on the cross. The Old Testament also gave prophetic explanations of what would take place on the cross. Crucifixion was not a common form of capital punishment in the Jewish culture. The Romans introduced it to Israel during the Roman Empire as a means to punish "slaves and criminals of the lowest order."[1] However, one thousand years before, David, Isaiah, and other Old Testament prophets had given detailed descriptions of what would one day bring the perfect atonement for their sins. In fact, this prophecy was made "about 800 years before the Romans adopted crucifixion. . . . To this day crucifixion is considered to be the most brutal form of execution."[2]

Old Testament Prophecy

1. The following exercise will give you a thorough comparison of these Old Testament passages and how Jesus fulfilled them as He went to the cross. Fill in the missing statements of Old Testament prophecy and New Testament fulfillment. (Bookmark Psalm 22, Matthew 27, and John 19 to help you find the passages and see the comparisons more quickly.)

	Prophecy	Fulfillment
Psalm 22:1 Matthew 27:46	My God, why hast thou forsaken me	Jesus' words on the cross
Psalm 22:2 Matthew 27:45	Cry in the day but don't hear me	Darkness on the earth for 3 hours
Psalm 22:7 Matthew 27:39	laugh me to scorn	as they passed by they reviled him wagging their heads
Psalm 22:8 Matthew 27:43	he trusted in the Lord that he would deliver him seeing he delighted in him	he trusted in God let him deliver him & he will have him for he said I am the Son of God
Psalm 22:14 Matthew 27:48	I am poured out like water, my bones are out of joint my heart is like wax it is melted in the midst of my bowels	One of them ran & took a sponge filled with vinegar put it on a reed & gave to him to drink

34

Psalm 22:15 John 19:28	My strength is dried up. my tongue cleaveth to my jaw & thou hast brought me into the dust of death	Jesus knowing all was accomplished said I thirst
Psalm 22:16 John 19:33–37; 20:25–27	dogs have compassed me - the assembly have enclosed me they pierced my hands & feet -	did not break legs pierced his side no bone should be broken
Psalm 22:17 John 19:23	tell my bones they look & stare upon me	They tore his robe into 4
Psalm 22:18 John 19:24	Cast lots for his garment	divided among soldiers
Psalm 34:20 John 19:34–46	Not one bone broken	pierced his side broke no bones
Zechariah 12:10 John 19:37	page 1023 OT	140 NT
Isaiah 53:9 Matthew 27:38	805 OT	39 NT
Isaiah 53:12 II Corinthians 5:21	806 OT	232 NT

New Testament Prophecy

The New Testament also forewarned the death Jesus would die. Shortly after Jesus was born, Mary and Joseph took Him to the temple for His dedication. While there , they met Simeon, a just and devout man who was allowed by God to live to see the Messiah.

Read Luke 2:32–35. What prophetic news did Simeon give to Mary and Joseph that day?

2. Match Simeon's prophecy with the verses that shows its fulfillment.

Simeon's Prophecy		*Fulfillment of Prophecy*
_B_	Jesus would be a light to Gentiles	A. I Peter 2:7–8
_A_	Jesus would be the glory of Israel	B. Acts 13:44–49
_E_	Jesus would be set for the fall and rising of many in Israel	C. John 19:25
_D_	Jesus would be a sign spoken against	D. Acts 28:22–24
_C_	Mary's soul would be pierced by a sword	E. Ezekiel 37:11–14

Let This Mind Be in You

Jesus also spoke of the death He would die as He ministered to the people of His day. He knew what lay before Him and began to prepare His disciples for that day. In Matthew 10:38–39, Jesus told His disciples, "And he that taketh not his cross, and followeth after me, is not worthy of me. He that findeth his life shall lose it: and he that loseth his life for my sake shall find it." He challenged His disciples to follow Him no matter where the path led. He wanted them to realize the cost of discipleship.

In Matthew 16:24, He told the apostles again that difficult times were ahead. They must not be surprised with what would come. He would go to Jerusalem and there He would suffer many things at the hand of the chief priests and scribes. He would give His life and be resurrected the third day. Peter rebuked the Lord and insisted that this should not happen. Jesus firmly reproved Peter, telling him he was not looking at these things as God was. Jesus then repeated the challenge for the disciples to deny themselves and take up their crosses and follow Him in surrendered obedience. To follow Him would involve a cross—the cross that He would carry and so would they.

3. What personal pain or loss has God asked you to carry?_____

_____

_____

4. How do you respond to these crosses in your life?_____

_____

_____

_____

5. Are you willing to obey God's Word and His will for you?_____

_____

_____

_____

6. What should you be doing differently in this area?_____

_____

_____

_____

❧ **Time for Prayer:** Spend some time in prayer asking God to give you a heart surrendered to all His will. Ask Him to help you obey even in the smallest matters.

❧ **Time to Memorize:** Continue to memorize Philippians 2:5–11.

From My Heart to Yours

The words of many hymns take us to the foot of the cross. One of the most loved hymns of the last century is "The Old Rugged Cross." The theme of the song came to Rev. George Bennard after an intense study to understand the full meaning of the cross. The writing of the words and music came years later, after a season of personal suffering in his life. The Lord helped Bennard understand the glories of the cross and then wanted him to know "the fellowship of His suffering" to be able to express the details of the cross with such passion. Ponder the words of this great hymn.

> On a hill far away stood an old rugged cross,
> The emblem of suffering and shame;
> And I love that old cross where the dearest and best
> For a world of lost sinners was slain.
>
> Oh, that old rugged cross, so despised by the world,
> Has a wondrous attraction for me;
> For the dear Lamb of God left His glory above
> To bear it to dark Calvary.
>
> To the old rugged cross I will ever be true,
> Its shame and reproach gladly bear;
> Then He'll call me some day to my home far away,
> Where His glory forever I'll share.
>
> So I'll cherish the old rugged cross,
> Till my trophies at last I lay down;
> I will cling to the old rugged cross,
> And exchange it some day for a crown.
>
> —*George Bennard*[3]

Are you living your life true to the cross? Are you gladly bearing the shame or reproach it may bring you? Are you cherishing and clinging to the Savior that hung on this cross for you?

Lesson 6
THE PROVISION
OF THE CROSS

Philippians 2:8
And being found in fashion as a man, he humbled himself,
and became obedient unto death, even the death of the cross.

The cross provided the payment for a debt we could never pay. No matter our past, our heritage, our intellect, or our goodness, we can do nothing to satisfy our debt of sin. It is not within our ability to do enough good to overcome our sinful hearts. Only the Lord Jesus, the Son of God, can satisfy what we owe. Matthew 20:28 tells us that Jesus Himself declared that He "came not to be ministered unto, but to minister, and to give His life a ransom for many." Our ransom was paid with the life of the Lord Jesus on the cross.

My Payment

Read the following verses and fill in the blanks with the missing words to better understand what Jesus did for us.

1. John 10:11—The good Shepherd gives His _Life_
   for His _sheep_

2. John 14:6—Jesus is the _truth_, _the way_
   and _life_. No man will come to the Father
   except _by me_

3. II Corinthians 5:21—Jesus was made to be _Sin_
for us that we might be made _righteous_ through
Him.

4. I Timothy 2:5–6—There is only _one God_ God
and only _One_ mediator between God and
man and that is _Christ Jesus_. He gave Himself as a
ransom for all of mankind.

My Place

We deserve to be punished for our own sins, but because of His great
love and mercy, He was willing to be our substitute. He took our
place on the cross. "As substitute, Christ took on Himself the sinner's
guilt and bore its penalty in the sinner's place."[1] This substitution
is often called "the vicarious Atonement, in which Christ died as a
substitute for sin."[2]

Read the verses to see for whom He died.

5. Romans 5:8—Christ died for _for us_

6. Ephesians 5:25—Christ died for _the Church_

7. Hebrews 2:9—Christ died for _every man_

My Pardon

ᘒ **Time in the Word: Read Psalm 103.**

Another thing we can learn from the cross is that forgiveness was
given because of Jesus' sacrifice. Because Jesus was willing to give His
life for us, you and I can know the joy of having our sins pardoned.
This word *pardon* was used throughout the Old Testament. In Isaiah 55:7, we are told, "our God . . . will abundantly pardon" and in
Jeremiah 33:8, God declares that He "will cleanse them from all their

iniquity, whereby they have sinned against me; and I will pardon all their iniquities, whereby they have sinned, and whereby they have transgressed against me."

The Hebrew word used in both verses refers to "the pardon extended to the sinner by God. . . . It is never used to denote that inferior kind and measure of forgiveness that is exercised by one man toward another."[3] Through this pardon, God reveals Himself to us. He shows us His love and goodness.

8. Match the verses with the characteristic that Jesus' pardon reveals. (Some verses will give more than one.)

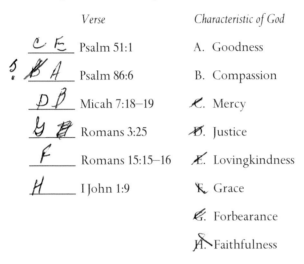

Verse	Characteristic of God
_C E_ Psalm 51:1	A. Goodness
_B A_ Psalm 86:6	B. Compassion
_D B_ Micah 7:18–19	C. Mercy
_G B_ Romans 3:25	D. Justice
_F_ Romans 15:15–16	E. Lovingkindness
_H_ I John 1:9	F. Grace
	G. Forbearance
	H. Faithfulness

In the New Testament, the words *remission* and *forgiveness* are often used for the same meaning as the Old Testament word *pardon*. This New Testament word means "forgiveness or pardon, of sins (letting them go as if they had never been committed), remission of the penalty."[4]

The first words Jesus spoke from the cross were words of pardon as He asked the Father to forgive those who had put Him there. Jesus wasn't referring just to the Roman soldiers or to the religious leaders that had accused Him of blasphemy. The sin of all mankind—past, present and future—made His death on the cross necessary. Jesus declared to the entire world that His purpose was to pardon all who would receive Him. Paul gives us a beautiful picture of what took place.

> And you, being dead in your sins and the uncircumcision of your flesh, hath he quickened together with him, having forgiven you all trespasses; blotting out the handwriting of ordinances that was against us, which was contrary to us, and took it out of the way, nailing it to his cross. (Colossians 2:13–14)

This "handwriting" that Paul refers to as an illustration of our sins "was an IOU signed by the debtor."[5] It pictures the law that no man could keep in spite of his best efforts. Man is then beholden to God—unable to reach the standard of God's perfection. Jesus graciously took that list of all our sins and took them upon Himself as He hung on the cross. Our sin debt was pardoned, graciously blotted out by the precious blood of our Lord.

As the Lord Jesus forgave, so should we. He is our perfect example, but other Bible characters also show us how to follow His pattern.

9. Read the accounts of some of these people, noting who forgave and who was forgiven.

Passage	Who Forgave?	Who Was Forgiven?
Genesis 14:21	Joseph	His brothers
I Samuel 24:1–8	*David*	*Saul*
II Samuel 19:18–23		*Shimei*
I Kings 1:50–53		
Acts 7:54–60		
II Timothy 4:6–16	*Paul*	*all*

Let This Mind Be in You

The Lord desires that we follow His example in the area of forgiveness. We all have people in our lives we must forgive. If we truly understand how Jesus forgives us, we should find it easier to forgive others.

10. Read the following verses and note how Jesus forgives us.

Psalm 103:12 _as far as the east is from the west_

II Samuel 12:13 _did it secretly_

Psalm 32:1 _deliver me in thy righteous_

Proverbs 28:13 _he who confess his sins & forsaketh them shall have mercy_

Isaiah 38:17 _Cast all my sins behind my back!_ 1016

Zechariah 3:4 _Clothe us with change of raiment._ 1016 ot

Hebrews 9:26 _he put away sin by the sacrifice of himself!_ 269 NT

43

11. According to Matthew 6:9–15, how does the Lord's forgiving you determine how you are to forgive others? _____

if we forgive men their trespasses your heavenly father will also forgive you!

12. Who in your life do you need to forgive? _____

all time

_____

_____

∽ **Time for Prayer:** Ask God to forgive you for whatever sins remain unconfessed in your heart and life. Thank Him for removing your sin as far as the east is from the west. Ask Him to give you the grace to forgive those who have hurt or wronged you.

∽ **Time to Memorize:** Continue to memorize Philippians 2:5–11.

From My Heart to Yours

Forgiveness is not something that comes naturally to us. Our sinful nature wants us to hold onto the pain that others cause us. We want to be repaid with apologies that meet our expected criteria of appropriateness. Our self-centeredness and pride lead us to believe we deserve far better than the offense.

I've heard many ask the question "Do I have to forgive them since they never have asked me to?" I wish I could say I never have posed such a query. But I can't deny it. I, too, have struggled with the timing of forgiveness. When did I have to forgive? I seemed determined to hang onto the unforgiving heart as long as possible. How awful it would be to forgive that person a minute sooner than I absolutely must.

When I stop to consider the forgiveness expressed to me by my Savior, I am ashamed that I have refused to do for others what He so willingly did for me. My sins against Him, which so greatly outnumber what anyone has ever done to me, put Him on the cross. He gave His life for my sins—providing the forgiveness my sins so desperately needed.

When I consider the timing of His provision for forgiveness, I am reminded that He died on the cross for my sins centuries before I was even born. His forgiving heart was ready and waiting to give His forgiveness the moment I asked. How can I not forgive someone immediately? As I remember God's loving forgiveness of me, I can then forgive others immediately. I can know the joy and freedom of forgiveness without bitterness. May we follow Paul's inspired instructions in Ephesians 4:32.

> Be ye kind one to another, tenderhearted, forgiving one another, even as God for Christ's sake hath forgiven you.

Lesson 7
THE PURSUIT OF THE CROSS

Philippians 2:8
**And being found in fashion as a man, he humbled himself,
and became obedient unto death, even the death of the cross.**

The message of salvation is found in the cross. In spite of man's attempts to develop his own way to God, all other plans fail to meet the criteria that God set. The gospel is the only essential message in history and the only vital issue of our lives. From the gospel all other facets of our lives fall into place. We need to "continually face up to . . . [our] own sinfulness and then flee to Jesus through faith in His shed blood and righteous life."[1] But what is this gospel and how does it apply to our lives? First Corinthians 15:3–4 states the gospel clearly.

> For I delivered unto you first of all that which I also received, *how that Christ died for our sins according to the scriptures; and that he was buried, and that he rose again the third day according to the scriptures* (emphasis added).

The gospel message is God's good news to all mankind: The Lord Jesus died on the cross for the sins of men, was buried, and three days later rose triumphant over sin and death. He took our punishment as He hung there on the cross. His shed blood satisfied the debt we owed—a debt we could never pay.

The power of the gospel goes beyond our salvation. It extends to our daily walk with the Lord. Through the power of the gospel we can live a life victorious over sin. The greater our understanding of what Christ did for us, the closer our walk to Him should be.

The Glory of the Cross

> But God forbid that I should glory, save in the cross of our Lord Jesus Christ, by whom the world is crucified unto me, and I unto the world. (Galatians 6:14)

In Galatians 6, Paul declares the glory of the cross. The issue was causing confusion among this group of believers. Many of the religious leaders were telling the Galatian Christians that they still needed to observe some of the Jewish laws to avoid persecution. "The gospel was somewhat tolerable for orthodox Jews if accompanied by circumcision and obedience to their law,"[2] so the Jews were teaching a salvation that mixed law with grace. Paul challenged these Christians to boldly declare, as he had, that salvation was in the work of Christ on the cross—not by any effort of their own. "[T]he cross itself had no power. Neither was it ever meant to be an idol, but it represents something so divine and powerful that the apostle Paul" reminded these believers to rejoice in what Jesus had done on the cross.[3] Paul realized he had nothing in himself to be proud of. All the glory should go to the Lord Jesus and His atoning work on the cross.

Read the following verses to learn more about the glory of the cross.

1. I Corinthians 1:17—Paul was sent to preach _the gospel_, not to baptize or to use words of his own wisdom.

2. Paul's preaching of the gospel would keep the message of the cross _lest the cross of Christ should be made of none effect_

3. I Corinthians 1:18—The cross is _foolishness_ to those who have not trusted Christ as Savior.

4. The cross is _power of God_ to those who are saved.

Christic Our Example

Christ Our Example

Time in the Word: Read I Peter 2:18–25.

Jesus' suffering is recorded as an example for us to follow. Committing Himself to the care and judgment of the Father, He willing endured the events that led to the cross. In I Peter 2, we read in detail of His pattern. Carefully consider how we should respond to suffering.

5. I Peter 2:18—We are to respond with a spirit of surrender not only to those in authority over us who are good to us but also to those who are _froward_.

6. I Peter 2:19—We will be commended (thankworthy), if we _endure_ grief for our beliefs and love for God.

7. I Peter 2:20—If we suffer for our faults, we should take the suffering patiently. But if we suffer for doing well, we are to respond with _patience_. This response is highly praised by God.

8. I Peter 2:21–23—As we understand the suffering the Lord Jesus endured for us, we realize we are called to endure suffering as He did. We are to "follow in His steps." What steps did Jesus take in response to the suffering He faced (*reviled* in the KJV means to attack verbally)?

a. _reviled not again_

b. _he threatened not_

c. _Committed himself to him that that judgeth righteousness_

d. _____

e. _____

49

9. I Peter 2:24–25—When we comprehend what the Lord Jesus did for us, we should be dead to _____*sin*_____, alive unto *righteousness*, and returned unto *the shepherd*.

Crucify Our Flesh

In Galatians 5:24, we are told, "they that are Christ's have crucified the flesh with the affections and lusts." When we trust Christ as Savior, we are to turn from our sin and live our lives in obedience to Him. The Holy Spirit comes to dwell within us and through His tutelage we learn to live a life that identifies us with Christ.

10. Study the following passages to learn what should be and should not be in our life if we are walking with our flesh truly crucified.

In Our Life	Passage	Not in Our Life
	Romans 6:6–13	
	Galatians 2:19–20	
	Galatians 5:19–24	

LET THIS MIND BE IN YOU

We are commanded in the Word to take up our cross and follow Christ. Each of us must carry a cross. These crosses come in different shapes and sizes and may even change throughout our lives, but all of us must be willing to take them up. Our "cross" can be something we must deal with because we have trusted the Lord as our personal Savior. This cross may be suffering or trials we must endure that someone unsaved would not experience. These crosses may also be trials and afflictions that anyone can face—even our unsaved neighbors. But as we deal with them, we should carry them with the grace and strength of God. He then is glorified through them. These crosses may ask me

> to content myself with a lowly and narrow sphere, when I feel that I have capacities for much higher work. . . . I may have to go on cultivating year after year, a field which seems to yield me no harvests whatsoever. I may be bidden to cherish kind and loving thoughts about someone who has wronged me. . . . I may have to confess my Master amongst those who do not wish to be reminded of Him and His claims. I may be called to "move among my race, and show a glorious morning face," when my heart is breaking.[4]

It is through these crosses that God makes Himself known to us as His children. He uses them to strengthen us and grow us that we might reflect His image more accurately. He desires that we lose our lives in service to Him. We are not worthy to be called His child if we are unwilling to follow Him. He desires first place in our lives, and it is through surrender that we learn to lift our cross and walk in His footsteps.

Read the following passages and answer these questions about taking up our cross.

11. Matthew 10:38–39—How does Jesus regard you if you are not willing to take up your cross and follow? *If we don't take up the cross we are not worthy of him*

51

12. What must you do to find the life God desires for you?_____

find our life

_____

13. Matthew 16:24—What three things did Jesus say had to happen for someone to truly "come after" Him?_____

deny self, take up the cross & follow him.

_____

14. Luke 9:23–26—How often are we to take up our cross?_____

daily

15. What do we have to gain by surrendering completely to the Lord?__ *Life*

_____

_____

֎ Time in Prayer: Ask the Lord to forgive you for any bitterness or resentment you may have toward the crosses you have been asked to carry. Thank Him for His work on the cross and for the privilege He has given you to fellowship with Him in suffering.

֎ Time to Memorize: Continue to memorize Philippians 2:5–11.

From My Heart to Yours

My son has played a variety of sports—baseball, soccer, basketball. His all-time favorite though is weightlifting. His interest began young; he asked for his first set of dumbbells at six. Those first 3-pound dumbbells have grown through the years to 100 pounds with a 550-pound squat being the most I've heard him speak of. While he and I have worked together on his snacks and meals to help with his conditioning, I've picked up some interesting facts.

Each day he works a different set of muscles. He knows the best combination of exercises with the precise amount of weight to push that muscle group to its maximum. But he also knows when to stop and how many days to rest that set of muscles before he works them again. He knows the nutritional content and quantity of food his body must have to maintain the regiment he demands it endure. This sport requires a discipline not often found in someone his age. Being a mom, I feel responsible to offer the cookies and cake that "every growing boys needs"; yet he usually refuses such offers to sustain his incredibly healthy diet.

Probably the most amazing thing he has taught me is that those muscles he's building are being built through a process of breaking. When he lifts the weights, the muscle breaks and through the rebuilding process becomes stronger. Who knew? I must have missed that day in biology class. I was under the impression that the muscles built new layers to explain their increased size. But breaking—I didn't realize.

So it is with my life. God knows what I need. He knows my limits; He remembers that I am but dust. He will not ask me to endure more than I can handle, yet He knows that to strengthen me, He must try me, stretch me. It's the breaking and suffering through pain and trials that God uses to make me stronger—more like the image of His Son.

GOD HATH HIGHLY
EXALTED HIM

Lesson 8
RESURRECTED IN POWER

Philippians 2:9
Wherefore God also hath highly exalted him

*M*any died on the cruel Roman cross. We have already learned that this Roman practice was one of the most horrific forms of capital punishment. Of all that died by this treacherous means, only One laid down His life—gave His life—and then arose victorious over death. That One, of course, was Jesus Christ.

Witnesses to the Resurrection

Time in the Word: Read Matthew 27:57–28:10.

After reading the account of Jesus' resurrection, answer the following questions.

1. Matthew 27:57–60—Jesus' body was carefully taken down from the cross. Where was it placed? *in a sepulchre that belonged to Joseph Arimathaea*

2. Matthew 27:62–66—Why did Pilate seal the stone and post guards at the tomb? *He was afraid the disciples would steal Jesus body & claim he had risen from the dead*

3. Matthew 28:1–4—Who awaited the women's arrival at the tomb? *an angel*

4. Matthew 28:5–7—What message did the women receive? *Fear not Jesus is not here he has risen*

5. Matthew 28:8–10—What happened on their way to tell the disciples the message? *Jesus met them & said Be not afraid & tell my brethren that they go into Gallilee and there shall they see me*

6. How is their response similar to what our response should be according to Philippians 2:10–11? *at the name of Jesus every knee shall bow and every tongue shall confess that Jesus Christ is Lord.*

7. Mark 16:11–14; Luke 24:10–12—How did the disciples receive the message brought to them by the women? *They didn't believe he had risen until they saw the cloth he was wrapped in.*

8. Luke 9:22; 8:32–33—Why should these events not have been a surprise to the disciples?

9. Read these passages to find out who Jesus appeared to after His resurrection.

Passage	People(s)	Location
Matthew 28:1, 9–10	Women	Jerusalem
Mark 16:9–11 John 20:11–18	*disciples* Mary Magdalene	at the sepulchure
Luke 24:13–35	Mary Magdalene Peter	Emmaus
John 20:19–25	disciples	
John 20:26–31	Thomas	
John 21:1–25	disciples	Tiberias
Acts 1:1–12	apostles	Olivet
I Corinthians 15:6	500 brethren	

Salvation Provided

J. Oswald Sanders says in *The Incomparable Christ*, "The doctrine of the resurrection is central in the Christian faith. . . . To deny it is to remove the keystone of the arch of Christianity. Without it, the crucifixion of our Lord would have been in vain, for it was the resurrection that validated and gave saving value to the atoning death."[1]

For I delivered unto you first of all that which I also received, how that Christ died for our sins according to the scriptures; and that he was buried, and that he rose again the third day according to the scriptures. (I Corinthians 15:3–4)

Without the resurrection of the Lord Jesus many things would be different! There would be . . .

No message of the gospel.

No victory over sin and death.

No satisfaction of the debt of sin.

No pardon and forgiveness of sin.

No salvation!

10. Read I Corinthians 15:14–19 and note what else would be different if Christ is not risen.

Verse 14 _preaching vain_
faith is vain

Verse 15 _false witness of God_

Verse 16 _____

Verse 17 _if Christ be not raised your faith is vain_

Verse 18 _those fallen asleep in Christ are perished_

Verse 19 _if in this life only we have hope in Christ we are of all men most miserable_

11. Read I Corinthians 15:20–22 to see what is true because He is risen.

Verse 20—He became the _first fruits_ of them that died.

Verses 21–22—By one man, _Adam_, came death; by One man, _Christ_, came life.

60

Spiritual Power

Jesus' resurrection not only provides salvation but it also gives spiritual power—power to live the Christian life in obedience. In Ephesians 1:18–20, Paul speaks of this power.

> The eyes of your understanding being enlightened; that ye may know what is the hope of his calling, and what the riches of the glory of his inheritance in the saints, and what is the exceeding greatness of his power to us-ward who believe, according to the working of his mighty power, which he wrought in Christ, when he raised him from the dead, and set him at his own right hand in the heavenly places.

This power is not limited to unique situations or certain callings. It is offered to all mankind for daily living. With Christ's conquering of sin and death, He provided the victory for all we face on a moment-by-moment basis.

This power is not forced upon us, but it must be appropriated. A loving Savior offers it with outstretched arms. As it is with salvation, so it is with His enabling power—we must reach out and take it for our own. This power, grace, enables us to walk the Christian life in obedient submission to God.

LET THIS MIND BE IN YOU

In Romans 6, Paul, through inspiration, teaches us about the victory and spiritual power that we each can experience because of the resurrection of Jesus Christ.

Read the verses from Romans 6 and fill in the blanks with the appropriate words to further explain this incredible power.

12. Romans 6:4–5—You should walk in _newness of life_ because of the resurrection.

13. Romans 6:6–10—You no longer have to serve _sin_

14. Romans 6:11—You should be _dead_ to sin.

15. Romans 6:13—You should commit yourself to _____ and not to _____ "as those that are alive from the dead."

Because Jesus was raised from the dead and now sits at the right hand of God the Father in heaven, what three things are you to understand according to Ephesians 1:15–23?

16. The _____ of His calling

17. The _____ of the glory of His _____ in the saints

18. The exceeding _____ of His _____ to us who believe

∿ Time for Prayer: Thank God for the victory and power that the resurrection provides for you. Confess as sin the areas of your life that you try to control in your own power.

∿ Time to Memorize: Continue to memorize Philippians 2:5–11.

From My Heart to Yours

In my determination to sort out and simplify my life, I decided to have a yard sale. While excavating through my mounds of boxed treasures, I found a plaque that had been a gift from a woman whom my children lovingly call "Grandma Mary." The words once again challenged my heart.

"The will of God will never lead you where the grace of God cannot keep you."

I have desired to walk in God's will since I was a little girl. Being saved at a very early age, I grew up wanting to know and obey God's will for my life. But there have been times that in spite of my confidence that I was in His will, I felt the burdens seemingly overwhelm me. During a particularly difficult time, I was unable to define God's grace. Yet this grace of God was what I heard would carry me through whatever I faced. I began a study—a searching—to understand what the sustaining grace of God really meant. I found many definitions, all of which described this commonly used biblical term. But my inquiring heart was settled when I put the various definitions into a nutshell: *God's grace is His enabling power that is given to me, His undeserving child.*

Now as I read the words on this forgotten little plaque, the meaning is deeper. I realize that He's proven it again and again in my life. I may not think He's keeping me in the midst of the trial, but never has He forsaken me, never allowed me to be crushed by the burden He has permitted to devastate me. He is there moment by moment—guiding me. Keeping me. Sustaining me. In spite of my resistance and fear. The words on this plaque are unchanged as they hang on the wall of my office. But the meaning is clearer to me now than ever before.

"The will of God will never lead me where the . . . [power] of God cannot keep me."

Lesson 9
RESURRECTED
WITH PROMISE

Philippians 2:9
Wherefore God also hath highly exalted him

One of the greatest blessings that resulted from the resurrection is the gift of an eternity in heaven to all who accept Jesus as Savior. When God breathed life into Adam's body, He gave to Adam and all mankind a soul that would live forever.

> And the Lord God formed man of the dust of the ground, and breathed into his nostrils the breath of life; and man became a living soul. (Genesis 2:7)

The living soul "stands for the entire person, and is not used in just the metaphysical, theological sense in which we tend to use the term soul today."[1] That living soul is the "part of us that is life."[2] Our soul will live forever somewhere.

Eternal Life

Since the Lord Jesus took our sins on the cross, we can claim His saving grace. With that salvation we are given eternal life—living forever in the presence of God—and escape eternal damnation. This "eternal life is more than an endless existence. It is a personal relationship with God."[3]

Read the following verses and fill in the missing words to learn about this unending life and relationship with God.

1. I John 5:11–13—_____God_____ is the source of eternal life (verse 11).

2. He who has the Son has _____life_____ and he who doesn't have the Son doesn't have _____life_____ (verse 12).

3. We can _____know_____ for certain that this eternal life is ours (verse 13).

4. Our eternal life is dependent upon a personal trust in _____God_____.

5. John 3:36—The _____wrath_____ of God is the outcome of one who doesn't receive the salvation provided through _____God_____.

6. John 11:25–26—Jesus is the _____Resurrection_____ and the _____life_____.

7. John 17:3—_____eternal_____ life is more than living somewhere forever. It is knowing God and Jesus, Whom God has sent.

Future Hope

Time in the Word: Read I Corinthians 15:20–23 and I Thessalonians 4:13–18.

Because Christ was raised from the dead, believers have the promise that they, too, will one day be resurrected. First Corinthians 15:20 refers to Jesus as the "first fruits"—the first of many to follow.

We as believers have a wonderful hope. First Thessalonians 4:13–18 is often used to explain this glorious expectation. It pictures for us the time when Christ will return and call believers to leave this earth behind and join Him for eternity in heaven. Paul wanted to be sure these people knew that they didn't have to be sorrowful as friends and loved ones left this life. Because Jesus died and rose again, believers will one day join Him in victory over death. After the bodies of the dead believers are resurrected and caught up with the Lord in the air, those who are alive will be caught up to meet Him.

8. Read I Thessalonians 4:16–17. List the order in which these events will occur.

Verse 16 _The Lord shall descend from heaven_

Verse 16 _The dead in Christ shall rise first_

Verse 17 _Those of us left shall be caught up together with them_

9. What does this truth give to Christians according to verse 18?

Comfort

LET THIS MIND BE IN YOU

For whatsoever things were written aforetime were written for our learning, that we through patience and comfort of the scriptures might have hope. (Romans 15:4)

God of Hope

Our God is a God of hope! In Romans 15 we read about the hope we have through the patience and comfort of the Scriptures (verse 4). We read a challenge to the Gentiles to trust, or hope, in God. Our greatest confidence is in God alone; "He is the author not the subject of" our hope.[4]

10. Match the verses with the truths about hope.

_C_ Even against all human reason we are to hope.   A. Colossians 1:27

_A_ The hope of glory is our certainty of heaven.   B. I Timothy 1:1

_E_ We are made heirs according to hope of eternal life.   C. Romans 4:18

_B_ The Lord Jesus is our Hope.   D. Romans 8:24

_D_ We are saved by hope.   E. Titus 3:7

_G_ Through the power of the Holy Spirit we are to abound in hope.   F. Romans 12:12

_F_ We are to rejoice in hope.   G. Romans 15:13

Are you hoping in the Lord? Answer the following questions honestly to evaluate your heart.

11. Can you say with confidence that your hope is in the Lord? Why or why not? _yes_ _____

_____

_____

_____

12. What areas of your life are you refusing to surrender to His control?

_____

_____

_____

13. Are you living each moment in your own strength or are you walking with the spiritual power that Paul spoke of in Ephesians and Romans? _____

_____

ᗡ Time for Prayer: Ask God to give you the courage to surrender every area of your life to His control. Ask Him to help you
realize that He is your Hope and Strength. Praise Him for the
eternal life He has given you through the Lord Jesus.

ᗡ Time to Memorize: Continue to memorize Philippians 2:5–11.

From My Heart to Yours

With my son about to graduate from high school, we began the
many celebrations that led up to that big day. Between special ads
for his yearbook and surprise video presentations for banquets and
receptions, I searched through the picture books for representative
pictures of years gone by. On one such hunt I explored a box of photos that dated back long before my son's birth. In fact, these treasures
went beyond my early years to those of my parents and grandparents.
I had forgotten that I even possessed these rare glimpses into my
heritage.

It was fun to see the memories captured by these black and white
photos. Time didn't just stand still for me; it seemed to drift back-
wards to days too often lost in the rush of my daily life. One thing
rang overwhelmingly true, however. The majority of these precious
people captured in these photos were no longer here on this earth.
They had gone on into eternity—some, many years ago. Although
these dear ones were family to me, to my children they were never
more than pictures from this forgotten collection.

My eyes even now fill with tears as I share with you these words.
But my tears are not ones of sorrow, although I do miss these dear
ones. My tears are more of anticipation to one day join them. With
the godly legacy these people left to me, I know that I shall see them
again when I join them in eternity. I know that I need not sorrow as
those who have no hope. For as these loved ones trusted the Lord
as their Savior, so have I. As they have left this life and have gone to
be with their Lord, one day so will I. I look forward to that reunion
when I will be with them not for a passing visit, but for eternity.

As precious as that reunion will be, it doesn't compare to seeing my resurrected Savior! He is the One my heart truly longs to see. When I leave this life, the Lord Jesus Himself will meet me in heaven, where He has been preparing a place just for me. All the cares of this life will be over. All the burdens, sorrow, and pain will be left behind as I step into His presence. What a day that will be—to see the glory of His face, to see the print of the nails in His hands, to kneel before Him, my Lord and Savior!

My Saviour First of All

When my life work is ended, and I cross the swelling tide,
When the bright and glorious morning I shall see;
I shall know my Redeemer when I reach the other side,
And His smile will be the first to welcome me.

Oh, the soul-thrilling rapture when I view His blessed face,
And the luster of His kindly beaming eye;
How my full heart will praise Him for the mercy, love, and grace,
That prepare me for a mansion in the sky.

Thro' the gates to the city in a robe of spotless white,
He will lead me where no tears shall ever fall;
In the glad song of ages I shall mingle with delight;
But I long to meet my Saviour first of all.

I shall know Him, I shall know Him,
And redeemed by His side I shall stand;
I shall know Him, I shall know Him
By the print of the nails in His hand.

—*Fanny Crosby*[5]

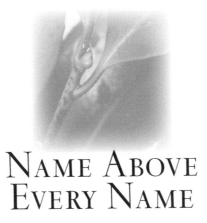

Name Above
Every Name

Lesson 10
EXALTED BY GOD

Philippians 2:9–11
Wherefore God also hath highly exalted him, and
given him a name which is above every name: that at
the name of Jesus every knee should bow, of things
in heaven, and things in earth, and things under the
earth; and that every tongue should confess that Jesus
Christ is Lord, to the glory of God the Father.

God's response to Jesus' surrender was to exalt Him. Three ways
are given in these verses that God lifts Jesus to the ultimate level of
glory.

1. Philippians 2:10—Every knee will___*Bow*___

_____

2. Philippians 2:11—Every tongue will *Confess that*
*Jesus Christ is Lord*_____

3. Philippians 2:11—Everyone will bring_____

_____

∾ **Time in the Word: Read Ephesians 1:15–23.**

   4. Read the following passages and note the ways in which God ex-
      alts Jesus and therefore brings glory to Himself.

Passage	Exaltation of Christ
Acts 2:32–33	Jesus exalted by the right hand of God
Ephesians 1:19–20	Raised from the dead and set on right hand of God
Ephesians 1:21	every name that is named not only in this world but that which is to come
Ephesians 1:22	put all things under his feet and gave him to be the head over all things to the church
Ephesians 1:23	The fullness of him that filleth all in all.
Hebrews 2:9	Crowned with glory & honor that he by the grace of God should taste death for every man
Hebrews 10:12	him as good as dead so many as the stars in the sky in multitude and as the sand which is by the sea shore innumerable

Given Him a Name

Another way in which God exalted the surrendered Lord was by giving Him a name "above, that is, 'more excellent than' every name."[1] One of the main purposes of Jesus' life here on earth was for Him to "declare" the Father to all (John 1:18). Through His life we learn Who God the Father is. Many times Jesus said that He had come to make His Father known to mankind.

> Then said they unto him, Where is thy Father? Jesus answered, Ye neither know me, nor my Father: if ye had known me, ye should have known my Father also. (John 8:19)

Many times Jesus said that He and the Father are one. When asked to explain Who He was in simple terms, Jesus clearly told the Jewish people that He is deity. He said in John 10:30, "I and my Father are one."

Jesus also taught that if we know Him, we know the Father as well. Philip asked the Lord Jesus to reveal the Father to the disciples in order to satisfy the confusion they had about Who God is. Jesus explained that to know Him is to know the Father.

> Jesus saith unto him, Have I been so long time with you, and yet hast thou not known me, Philip? He that hath seen me hath seen the Father; and how sayest thou then, Shew us the Father? (John 14:9)

In his book on the divine character and attributes of the Lord Jesus, Randy Jaeggli states, "Since Christ and the Father are one . . . everything the Old Testament says about the character of Yahweh is also true of Christ."[2] This statement challenged me to prove it. I have studied the Old Testament names of God and how God's character is revealed through those names. I found it amazingly apparent that Jesus does fulfill every Old Testament name and attribute of God—proving repeatedly that He and the Father are truly one.

5. Take time to ponder each section of the following exercise. The Old Testaments names will encourage you as you are reminded of Who God is; the New Testament passages will show the overwhelming proof of Jesus' identity as Messiah.

Old Testament Passage	Name/Position	New Testament Passage	Name/Position
Genesis 2:4	Creator (Elohim)	John 1:2–4	Creator
Genesis 15:2	*abram/ steward*	John 20:16	*Mary / master*
Genesis 22:13, 14	*abraham*	Matthew 6:31–32	*Jesus*
Exodus 3:14	*God*	John 8:58	*Jesus I am*

Old Testament Passage	Name/Position	New Testament Passage	Name/Position
Exodus 15:26	*Lord God Healer*	Matthew 9:12–13	*Jesus Physician*
Deuteronomy 18:15–22	*Lord*	John 4:25–26	*Jesus*
Deuteronomy 18:15	*Lord Prophet*	Acts 3:20, 22	*Jesus*
Judges 6:24	*Gideon*	John 14:27	*God*
Psalm 2:7	*Lord*	Matthew 3:17	*God*
Psalm 23:1	*Lord*	John 10:11	*Jesus*
Psalm 110:4	*Lord Priest*	Hebrews 5:5–6	*God Jesus*
Isaiah 9:7	*Lord*	Luke 1:32–33	*God*
Isaiah 45:21	*Lord God*	John 4:42	*Jesus*
Isaiah 53:7	*Lord*	John 1:29, 36	*John & Jesus* *Lamb of God*
Zechariah 9:9	*King Jesus*	John 18:33	*Pilate Jesus*

Let This Mind Be in You

6. From the list above choose several names of God and determine how your life—your actions or decisions—will be different today in light of Who He is.

Name of God _____

How should that affect your life today? _____

_____

_____

Name of God_____

How should that affect your life today?_____

_____

_____

Name of God_____

How should that affect your life today?_____

_____

_____

Name of God_____

How should that affect your life today?_____

_____

_____

ᕃ **Time for Prayer: Spend time in prayer exalting God through praising His many names. Thank Him for revealing Himself to us through His names.**

ᕃ **Time to Memorize: Continue to memorize Philippians 2:5–11.**

From My Heart to Yours

Over the past years I have learned to claim the truths of Who God is by focusing on His names. The meanings and applications of His names have given me a greater understanding of my God. Through them I have learned that He is the God of comfort and courage, of strength and security, of guidance and grace, and of provision and promise. It would take an entire study to look closely at these revealing names, and I challenge you to take the exercises in this section to learn more about the names of the Lord God.

We become accustomed to the phrases "in His name" or "for His name's sake" and we fail to consider what they mean. Do you realize all that is promised us through His name? Prayerfully consider the following verses.

Neither is there salvation in any other: for there is none other name under heaven given among men, whereby we must be saved. (Acts 4:12)

And whatsoever ye shall ask in my name, that will I do, that the Father may be glorified in the Son. If ye shall ask any thing in my name, I will do it. (John 14:13–14)

And every one that hath forsaken houses, or brethren, or sisters, or father, or mother, or wife, or children, or lands, for my name's sake, shall receive a hundredfold, and shall inherit everlasting life. (Matthew 19:29)

For whosoever shall call upon the name of the Lord shall be saved. (Romans 10:13)

Lesson 11
WORSHIPED BY ALL

Philippians 2:9–11
Wherefore God also hath highly exalted him, and
given him a name which is above every name: that at
the name of Jesus every knee should bow, of things
in heaven, and things in earth, and things under the
earth; and that every tongue should confess that Jesus
Christ is Lord, to the glory of God the Father.

God exalted the Lord Jesus. He honored His obedience and accepted His provision for sin through His death and resurrection. We, as mankind, have the continual responsibility to show our admiration and obedience to the Lord Jesus by worshiping Him.

In Philippians 2:10–11 we read that worship involves every knee bowing and every tongue confessing that Jesus is Lord. The adjective *every* is used in both instances to show the extent that man will show Him this respect and glory.

Every Knee Shall Bow

Time in the Word: Read Romans 14:9–13.

One day all of mankind will stand before God. He will be the perfect, holy, righteous Judge, Who demands an accounting of each man's thoughts and deeds. There will be two separate judgments for individuals. One will be for those who have trusted Christ as Savior. Their judgment will not determine their eternal destiny because their eternity is secure in Christ's work on the cross, which they received when they were saved in this life. Let's look first at this judgment.

Romans 14:9–13 explains this judgment, which is often referred to as the judgment seat of Christ. Refer to this passage to answer the following questions.

1. Christ's death and resurrection makes Him Lord over whom (verse 9)? *the dead & living*

2. Do we have the right to judge those around us? Why or why not? *No*

3. Who is exempt from this judgment (verse 10)? *No one*

4. Of whom will we give an account (verses 11–12)? *To God*

5. What are we to judge (verse 13)? *That no man put a stumbling block or an occasion to fall in his brother's way*

First Corinthians 3:11–15 also speaks of this judgment seat of Christ. Although this judgment does not determine a person's salvation, all who have trusted in Christ as Savior will be judged and rewarded for faithfully and obediently serving Christ.

Read I Corinthians 3:11–15 to answer the following questions.

6. On what foundation have these lives been built (verse 11)? *Jesus Christ*

7. List the six building materials under the proper categories.

Temporal	Eternal
Reviled	bless
defamed	entreat
persecuted	suffer

8. What do the building materials represent? _The_
filth of the earth _and used as a_
Christian

9. What will God use to reveal the value of the works?
fire will test each our work Gospel

10. If the work "abides," what shall the person receive?
~~Rec Receive a~~
Receive a Reward

11. Do we deserve this on our own worth or merit? _No_

12. What further explanation do these verses give?

I Corinthians 9:16–17 _Woe unto o me if_
I don't preach the gospel. do willing a
reward, against my will a dispensation
of the gospel is committed
II John 8 _____

_____

_____

13. If our works burn, what will we lose? _lose your reward_

All those who die without trusting in Christ as Savior will stand
before the Lord at the judgment called the great white throne judgment. Those who refused to receive Him as Savior in this life will face
Him as Judge.

Revelation 20:11–15 gives us an account of this judgment. Read this passage carefully to answer the questions.

14. Describe the throne and the Judge. *White throne*
God y' oldy

15. Who will stand before this Judge (verse 12)? *Everyone*

16. What book will be opened (verse 12)? *book of life*

17. What is recorded in this book for which these people will be judged (verse 13)? *their works*

18. What is the fate of those not found in the Book of Life (verse 15)?
Cast into the lake of fire

Every knee shall bow to Him!
As Savior or as Judge!
In praise or in condemnation!
In rejoicing or in fear!

Every Tongue Confess

Every woman that has ever lived will find that she will have to give testimony to the fact that Jesus is God. Deuteronomy 6:13 commands us to "fear . . . serve . . . swear by his name." As we realize all that the Lord Jesus is and all that He has done for us, we cannot help but lift our hearts in praise. He is our Lord and all praise is His, "to the glory of God the Father."

LET THIS MIND BE IN YOU

In Jeremiah 9:23–24, Jeremiah instructs us in how to give glory to God. Read this passage and answer the following questions.

19. In what three things should man not glory or boast?

a. _____wise_____ man not glory in his _____Wisdom_____

b. _____mighty_____ man not glory in his _____might_____

c. _____rich_____ man not glory in his _____riches_____

Do you glory in these?_____

20. In what two things should man glory or boast?

a. That he _____ God

b. That he _____ God

Do you glory in these?_____

21. What three things do we learn about God? God displays

a. _____

b. _____

c. _____

And in these He_____

_____

22. What does He deserve to be? Match the correct answer with the verse.

___C___ Matthew 23:8, 10   A. Given all glory

___D___ John 13:13   B. Lord of the living and the dead

___B___ Romans 14:9   C. Master

___A___ I Corinthians 1:31   D. Master and Lord

23. What changes in your relationship to God do you need to make with His help?_____

_____

_____

_____

_____

83

- Time for Prayer: During your prayer time today, confess any area of your life that is not giving Him the glory He deserves. Spend some time praising and thanking God for Who He is.

- Time to Memorize: Continue to memorize Philippians 2:5–11.

From My Heart to Yours

> Then I went down to the potter's house, and, behold, he wrought a work on the wheels. And the vessel that he made of clay was marred in the hand of the potter: so he made it again another vessel, as seemed good to the potter to make it. Then the word of the Lord came to me, saying, O house of Israel, cannot I do with you as this potter? saith the Lord. Behold, as the clay is in the potter's hand, so are ye in mine hand. (Jeremiah 18:3–6)

My college art appreciation teacher was a very gifted woman whose ability in the field of art was celebrated. Her love for art must have made our class of art-ignorant education majors a difficult chore at best. The principles she introduced were no doubt boringly basic to someone so knowledgeable, yet she diligently presented the material to us with the simplicity required.

One day she took us into the room with a potter's wheel and proceeded to demonstrate the art of throwing a pot. The grace and skill she displayed was phenomenal. The clay responded to her every touch. Her hands were the masters of the clay and under their precise pressure the shapeless lump was transformed before our eyes into a useful vessel.

There are times, as Jeremiah reminds us, that the clay refuses to respond to the potter's touch and is cast aside and deemed worthless. It is of no value to the potter or the one needing a vessel. But the clay that is submissive to the potter's touch will be a trophy of glory to the craftsman. The results will be a vessel that gives credit to its maker.

So it is in our lives. When we willingly submit to the will of God for us, we will become a vessel that brings glory and praise to our God. Our worship cannot begin when we enter our church at the appointed hour of services, but our adoration of Him must be moment by moment. There is no greater way to give Him His rightful adoration than by surrendering ourselves to Him in complete obedience.

What kind of clay are you?

MY LIFE SURRENDERED

Lesson 12
MY LIFE SURRENDERED—
HIS LIFE EXALTED

Philippians 1:20–21
**Christ shall be magnified in my body, whether it be by life,
or by death. For to me to live is Christ, and to die is gain.**

As we have studied the life of the Lord Jesus, we have looked at His life from eternity past as He dwelt in heaven. We have seen how He surrendered to be born and live as man on this earth and have walked with Him through the land of Israel ministering to all He came in contact with. We have seen how He surrendered to the cruel death of the cross and rose again. But just to know academically the details of our Lord's example may leave us unchanged. Each lesson has challenged us to apply these truths to our daily lives, but let's look at one final application.

In order for us to fully surrender to Him, we must make a decision not only to surrender to His complete control but also to exalt Him. This degree of surrender will bring changes to our daily lives. We will put Him as the center of our thoughts and plans. He will be our first and foremost consideration in all we do and say. He will be our source of joy and strength.

Many Bible characters learned to walk this surrendered walk, but we will look at just two. You may want to study others from the

Bible who exemplify this same attitude and dedication. Let's begin with John the Baptist.

John the Baptist

John the Baptist was the one the prophets had predicted would prepare the way for Jesus' earthly ministry. Although John had a large following, he openly told the people that he was not the awaited Messiah. When Jesus came to the Jordan River to be baptized, John boldly declared Him to be the Lamb of God, the promised Messiah. After Jesus' ministry was underway and John's drew to a close, John clearly surrendered all his loyalty and reverence to the Lord.

℘ **Time in the Word: Read John 3:27–30.**

After you have read these verses, carefully answer the following questions about John's declaration of Who Jesus was.

1. From where do we each receive our abilities (verse 27)?_____

   _____*from heaven*_____

2. Since God is an all-knowing, perfect God, what should our attitude be toward our abilities in comparison to the abilities of others?_____

   _____

   _____

   _____

3. Do we determine the success or failure of our efforts when we obediently and faithfully do what God has called us to? Explain.

   _____*yes*_____

   _____

   _____

   _____

   _____

4. What had John taught his followers about God's purpose for and explanation of his ministry (verse 28)?

I am not the Christ, but that I am sent before him

5. What made John joyful (verse 29)?

To hear the bridegroom's voice
Bridegroom's

6. When John saw Jesus, what did he realizes must happen (verse 30)_

he must decrease

7. Will increasing our knowledge and love for Christ be a difficult arrangement? Explain. _I think no yes. There is to much self in us._

8. What should always be our underlying goal? _to be more like Jesus_

Paul the Apostle

As you read Acts 9:1–22, note that Paul was a man of much prestige within the religious community of his day. He had trained at the feet of Gamaliel, the most renowned Jewish teacher at that time. He enjoyed a social status because of his Roman citizenship. His zeal for persecuting the early believers was matched only by his fervor for Christ after his salvation. Paul's conversion is a dramatic picture of surrender and the changes that can result.

9. Fill in the blanks to summarize the account of Saul's conversion.

Saul, whose name later became _Paul_, threatened and murdered the followers of _the Lord_. Saul requested written permission from the _high priest_ to bring the Christians from _Damascus_ to Jerusalem to be dealt with for their beliefs. On the way to _Damascus_, a light suddenly shone on Saul and caused him to fall down. Saul heard the _voice_ of the Lord Jesus, Who asked Saul why he was _persecuting_ Him. Saul knew who was speaking to Him and asked the Lord what He would have him do. The men with Saul were not aware of all that was happening and stood _speechless_. Saul went into Damascus and awaited the arrival of _Ananias_. God sent _ananais_ to restore Saul's _sight_ and to give him instructions for the _plan_ God had for him. Saul went to the _synagogues_ and preached that Jesus is truly the _Son of God_.

Paul's unparalleled ministry for God began with his surrender to the Lord on the way to Damascus. Throughout Paul's life of service he had a heart of submission. His dedication was unsurpassed as he proclaimed the message of the gospel to Jew and Gentile alike.

Read Philippians 2:20–21 to answer the following questions about Paul's approach to a surrendered life.

10. What should be the Christian's greatest desire (verse 20)?_____

To be like Jesus

11. How is Christ magnified in our bodies?

Romans 12:1 _a living sacrifice, holy acceptable unto God, which is your reasonable service_

Romans 6:13 *Yield yourselves to God, as those that are alive from the dead and your members as instruments of righteousness unto God —*

12. With what attitude are we to magnify Christ?_____

_____

13. How can we magnify Christ with our life?_____

_____

_____

_____

With our death?_____

_____

_____

14. How would you compare Paul's approach to ministry with that of John the Baptist's?_____

_____

_____

15. What should both life and death be counted to the Christian (verse 21)?_____

_____

16. Was Paul so ready to die and be with the Lord that he became impatient with life (verses 22–25)?_____

Explain._____

_____

_____

_____

_____

Christlike surrender is seen in these men as well as in other Bible characters. What about you? Are you surrendered to the Lord? Do you have a mind as He did to totally fulfill God's will? God desires each of us to be a living sacrifice. After these lessons of looking at the life of the Lord Jesus, how can we be satisfied to be anything less than fully surrendered to our Lord Jesus!

LET THIS MIND BE IN YOU

17. What have you learned from the life of the Lord Jesus and His surrender? As you consider each phrase of Philippians 2:9–11, remind yourself of the example Jesus set for you to follow.

Obedient unto Death

Jesus' example of surrender_____

_____

_____

_____

What must I do?_____

_____

_____

_____

Even the Death of the Cross

Jesus' example of surrender_____

_____

_____

_____

What must I do?_____

_____

_____

_____

God Hath Highly Exalted Him

Jesus' example of surrender_____

_____

_____

_____

What must I do?_____

_____

_____

_____

Name Above Every Name

Jesus' example of surrender_____

_____

_____

_____

What must I do?_____

_____

_____

_____

Let This Mind Be in You

Summarize the mind of Jesus_____

_____

_____

_____

What must I do?_____

_____

_____

_____

His Life Exalted

Summarize what you should be doing to exalt the Lord Jesus.

_____

_____

_____

18. What areas of your life have you surrendered more completely to Him as a result of this study?

_____

_____

_____

_____

∾ **Time to Memorize: Review Philippians 2:5–11.**

∾ **Time for Prayer: Take time in prayer to thank God for what He's done for you and for the victory you can have in Him. Take time to exalt the Lord as your Savior and Friend. Determine to daily surrender all to Him.**

From My Heart to Yours

This concludes our study of *A Life Surrendered—A Life Exalted*. We have seen how the Lord Jesus surrendered when He came to this earth. He became man, humbly became the example of a servant, and became obedient to the death on a Roman cross. But death could not keep Jesus. He arose victorious! With that resurrection came victory for all who call on His name.

We must each ask ourselves if our lives are truly surrendered to the Lord. We all are yielding daily to something or someone. Who is in control of your life? It may be that you are following your own self-centered desires and dreams. You may be concerned only for what will benefit you or those closest to you. If we are to follow the example of the Lord Jesus, we must set aside our plans and purposes and give ourselves totally to Him. We must be willing to do whatever He asks of us.

Where are you today? Have you first of all surrendered to the Lord Jesus as your Savior? Are you daily walking in obedience to His Word? Are you willing to obey Him no matter the cost? He desires that each one of us give ourselves daily and completely to His control. God wants 100 percent of us! He will not force us to surrender to Him but will instead draw us to Himself by His love and goodness. Without giving Him our lives as living sacrifices, we fall short of complete surrender.

Even in the midst of our most difficult times, we can know that He is our God; He understands; He will never leave us; He will never forsake us. God is in control and He will bring about His perfect will.

It is from surrender that our obedience and trust are developed. It is from a heart of surrender that we can glorify our Lord and Savior. Are you exalting Him as He deserves? Are you praising Him moment by moment for His goodness and grace to you no matter your circumstances?

> Let this mind be in you, which was also in Christ Jesus: who, being in the form of God, thought it not robbery to be equal with God: but made himself of no reputation, and took upon him the form of a servant, and was made in the likeness of men: and being found in fashion

as a man, he humbled himself, and became obedient unto death, even the death of the cross. Wherefore God also hath highly exalted him, and given him a name which is above every name: that at the name of Jesus every knee should bow, of things in heaven, and things in earth, and things under the earth; and that every tongue should confess that Jesus Christ is Lord, to the glory of God the Father. (Philippians 2:5–8)

Spend time praising and thanking the Lord for all He is and all He's done for you. Thank Him for His example of surrender. Promise daily to give your life in surrendered obedience to Him. Let the words to this hymn be the song of your heart today!

May your life be surrendered and His name be exalted!

I Surrender All

All to Jesus I surrender,
All to Him I freely give;
I will ever love and trust Him,
In His presence daily live.

All to Thee, my blessed Saviour,
I surrender all.

—*Judson W. Van DeVenter*[1]

Notes

Lesson 2: The Surrender to Betrayal

[1]*King James Study Bible* (Nashville: Thomas Nelson Publishers, 1981), 1647.

Lesson 3: The Surrender to a Trial

[1]J. Oswald Sanders, *The Incomparable Christ* (Chicago: Moody Press, 1971), 141.

[2]Sanders, 142.

[3]Ron Hamilton, "Not My Will," *Majesty Hymns* (Greenville, S.C.: Majesty Music, 1996).

Lesson 4: The Prophecy of the Cross, Part 1

[1]*King James Study Bible*, 15.

Lesson 5: The Prophecy of the Cross, Part 2

[1]John R. Cross, *The Stranger on the Road to Emmaus* (Olds, Alberta, Can.: GoodSeed International, 2002), 228.

[2]Cross, 229.

[3]George Bennard, "The Old Rugged Cross," *Worship and Service Hymnal* (Carol Stream, Ill.: Hope Publishing Company, 1973), 63.

Lesson 6: The Provision of the Cross

[1]Sanders, 150.

[2]*King James Study Bible*, 1738.

[3]*The New Strong's Expanded Dictionary of the Words in the Hebrew Bible* (Nashville: Thomas Nelson Publishers, 2001), 197.

[4]*The New Strong's Expanded Dictionary of the Words in the Greek New Testament* (Nashville, Thomas Nelson Publishers, 2001), 48.

[5]*King James Study Bible,* 1864.

Lesson 7: The Pursuit of the Cross

[1]Jerry Bridges, *The Discipline of Grace* (Colorado Springs: NavPress, 1973), 58.
[2]*King James Study Bible*, 1824.
[3]Beth Moore, *Jesus the One and Only* (Nashville: Broadman and Holman, 2002), 264.
[4]Mrs. Charles E. Cowman, *Streams in the Desert*, quoting Alexander Smellie (Grand Rapids: Zondervan, 1965), 286.

Lesson 8: Resurrected in Power

[1]Sanders, 211.

Lesson 9: Resurrected with Promise

[1]*King James Study Bible*, 9.
[2]*King James Study Bible*, 9.
[3]*King James Study Bible*, 1645.
[4]*The New Strong's Expanded Dictionary of the Words in the Greek New Testament*, 86.
[5]Fanny J. Crosby, "My Saviour First of All," *Worship and Service Hymnal* (Carol Stream, Ill.: Hope Publishing Company, 1973).

Lesson 10: Name Above Every Name

[1]*King James Study Bible*, 1851.
[2]Randy Jaeggli, *More like the Master* (Greenville, S.C.: Ambassador International, 2004), 268.

Lesson 12: My Life Surrendered—His Life Exalted

[1]Judson W. Van DeVenter, "I Surrender All," *Worship and Service Hymnal* (Carol Stream, Ill.: Hope Publishing Company, 1973).